WAIT,
STAY
or GO

WAIT, STAY, or GO

Following the Voice of God

DONNA R. MARTIN

NEW YORK

LONDON • NASHVILLE • MELBOURNE • VANCOUVER

WAIT, STAY *or* GO

Following the Voice of God

Published in New York, New York, by Morgan James Publishing. Morgan James is a trademark of Morgan James, LLC. www.MorganJamesPublishing.com

Morgan James BOGO™

A **FREE** ebook edition is available for you or a friend with the purchase of this print book.

CLEARLY SIGN YOUR NAME ABOVE

Instructions to claim your free ebook edition:
1. Visit MorganJamesBOGO.com
2. Sign your name CLEARLY in the space above
3. Complete the form and submit a photo of this entire page
4. You or your friend can download the ebook to your preferred device

ISBN 9781631954603 paperback
ISBN 9781631954610 ebook
Library of Congress Control Number:
2020951521

Cover Design by:
Rachel Lopez
www.r2cdesign.com

Interior Design by:
Melissa Farr
melissa@backporchcreative.com

Morgan James PUBLISHING Builds with... Habitat for Humanity® Peninsula and Greater Williamsburg

Morgan James is a proud partner of Habitat for Humanity Peninsula and Greater Williamsburg. Partners in building since 2006.

Get involved today! Visit
MorganJamesPublishing.com/giving-back

I dedicate this book to every woman who is contemplating divorcing her husband.

Although we may not all be in the exact same situation or experiencing the same issues, we can all relate to the pain we may endure while in this period of indecision. Some of us are still living with our husbands and are disconnected emotionally. Others may be physically separated from our husbands. No matter what your situation may be at this moment, you may still be experiencing some of the same struggles that others face. We all face the same question: "What do I do now?"

By seeking God and waiting on Him for the answers we need, which may not be the same answer for each of us, we will find the peace, clarity and understanding needed to make the right decision.

I pray that this book will help you to learn how to wait on God to receive all the answers that you need. I pray that by sharing the pain behind the purpose for this book that you are encouraged to wait on God; so, that no matter the outcome, He above all else is glorified. I also pray that you receive the understanding needed from God concerning your unique situation so that while you wait, you can gain the wisdom needed to know the answer to the following questions:

God, do I continue to wait?
Do I stay or is it time for me to go?

Table of Contents

Acknowledgments

First, I want to honor and thank God for giving me the strength to make it through the trials and tests I had to go through; for having the patience to wait on me until I realized it was Him that I truly desired and needed more than anyone or anything else, and for giving me the courage to write this book.

I want to thank Lady J, the First Lady of New Life COGIC, for her encouragement and support, and for helping me to find the purpose in my pain and the reason for this book.

I want to thank Prophetess Lois Russell and Bakeba C. Raines (Edits by Bakeba) for so graciously agreeing to edit my book. I also want to say thank you to Morgan James Publishing Company for seeing the value of helping others in my book and your willingness to publish it.

A special thank you to both of my accountability partners: Candace B Woods, author of "While I Wait" and Tanika Garrett, visionary of StepMOMents for encouraging me to keep pressing and for not leaving me behind when I would drag my feet.

I would also like to thank all of the friends that encouraged me along the way.

Foreword

When Donna Martin approached me about being one of the editors of her first book, I could feel her excitement about this new "baby" that she was about to birth. I could also feel her sincerity of purpose in putting into words one of the most painful experiences of her life. Even though I had known Donna for several years, I had no idea of the severity of her test. It never showed in her faithfulness to our church, in her unbridled worship, in her compassionate intercession for others or in her beautiful smile. The phrase, "You don't look like what you've been through" is aptly applied in speaking of Donna Martin.

In the pages of this book, the story of Donna's marriage unfolds with an unselfish transparency that is sure to touch the hearts of those who read it; but even more important to the author, this book will serve as a source of comfort and wisdom for those who are experiencing the pain of a troubled marriage. At its core, *Wait, Stay or Go: Following the Voice of God* delivers a fervent message of hope and encourages the reader to seek a deeper relationship with God, trusting that He has the answer for even the most desperate situations.

I believe that true ministry is always made more powerful when it is based on firsthand experience and when it is firmly anchored in God's word and love.

This book certainly is a tool of ministry. It is destined to be a blessing to those who experience it.

And remember, as I said at the beginning, this is Donna's first book.

Co-Pastor Lois G. Russell
New Life COGIC-Annex 5

Preface

I decided to start a blog and write this book because I became increasingly concerned about the number of marriages that I saw being destroyed by the enemy. I decided to be transparent about my own marriage and my experiences so that I could help other couples. I truly believe that too many people give up too easily on their marriages instead of seeking God for direction and instruction.

I believe it is time for us to save our marriages through spiritual warfare using the Word of God to fight the enemy who desires nothing more than to destroy them.

Introduction

MANY WOMEN HAVE experienced their husbands leaving them, either literally or figuratively. But how did they handle the situation? What were they saying to themselves or to others? Or were they saying nothing at all? How did they feel? Were they glad that their husbands had left them or were they just ready to give up? Were they wondering, "Why me", and becoming angry with and blaming God? Did they decide to take up with Jody down the street? Did they say, "Forget this mess." "I don't have to take this. I'm going to see my lawyer!"

OR did they choose to wait and hear from God before they made any decisions?

I wrote this book after my own experience of having to choose to wait and hear from God when making one of the hardest choices in my life—should I walk away from my marriage. With this book, I want to encourage women that are struggling in their marriages to pursue God for direction. This book outlines steps that we, as women, should take when making any decision but especially when we are making decisions regarding our covenant with our God—our marriages.

I have included Notes pages throughout the book. You can document, on those pages, your thoughts and emotions that may come up as you read through these steps that I went through to come to the realization that our most important relationship here on Earth is our relationship with our Father who is in heaven, our God.

My Journey Begins

LET ME SHARE a little of my story with you. I began this journey of waiting on God at the beginning of 2013.

I truly felt that my husband was sent to me by God. He was a good provider, caring, kind-hearted and affectionate. He seemed to have all of the qualities most women tend to look for in Mr. Right. I had prayed and I knew I had heard from God. After nine months of dating, I married my husband. I already had three children. My husband didn't have any.

Since I was older, he said he felt that he would be fine if we never had any children together. He knew that I might not be able to have any more children because years prior to our meeting I had gotten my tubes tied. But because I loved him, I went through a tubal reversal in order for us to try to have children. After my surgery, I became pregnant right away, but I lost the baby.

As we watched my children begin to have more children, my husband's desire to have a child of his own increased. He became a substitute teacher just to be around children. It was painful for me to know that we had not been able to have a child, but it was even more painful to know that he began to feel stuck and very unhappy. I knew that, up to this point, I was unable to become pregnant nor do anything about it. If we were going to have a child, God would have to perform a miracle. I felt that if God would just do this one thing for me, ALL would be right with the world and we would live happily ever after.

We continued to try to have a baby. We tried IVF (in-vitro fertilization) which unfortunately was also unsuccessful. We continued to try to have a baby naturally. After eight more years of unsuccessfully attempts, my husband began to feel that if he was going to have a chance to have the baby that he so desperately desired, it would have to be with someone else—someone younger. I felt that he loved me and I knew I loved him, but at that time I didn't know if love would be enough.

… and eventually it wasn't enough.

My husband left me after being married for nine years. It was at this point I began my "Wait".

For a long time, I did not share with anyone that my husband had left. Why? Because I didn't want to hear "What they would do if it were them" or "What they wouldn't put up with if it were them". By the time that I did share, l realized that I had come to a place that all I wanted to hear was what God had to say, not just about the situation with my husband, but about everything concerning my life. My life continued and my husband was still a part of it. Although he had left our home, we still interacted with each other, attending family functions together and spending time with each other. In May of 2014, we were expecting again. Unfortunately, by the time I learned that I was pregnant, I was miscarrying again. I would have had twins this time. I was devastated. I knew that my husband was too. I felt like he was going to do something irrational. And he did.

In August 2014, I had a dream about my husband. He was standing in the middle of a field at the top of a hill. In the dream, I walked up to him and said something in his ear. I could not hear or understand what I said, but he began to cry uncontrollably. I shared the dream with one of my closest friends and told her that God revealed to me that my husband was not crying because something was wrong with him; he was crying because he had done something that he knew was going to hurt me. I was right.

On February 25, 2015, my husband called me and said that he had something he needed to tell me. I knew in my heart and soul that it wasn't good. I prayed the entire evening as I waited for him to come talk to me. I told God, "God, I know this isn't going to be good for me." Again, I was right. He came to tell me that he might have a son; however, he wasn't sure the child was his and he was having a paternity test done as soon as possible. What a kick in the gut that was for me. There was no way possible for me to see anything good that could come out of this situation. All it did was make me think about the baby I had lost and that our baby would have been born around the same time as his son or a little earlier. The hurt and pain I felt cannot be put into words nor was there any medication that could relieve it. To know that this situation only happened out of the pain he felt for losing our babies months before, gave me no relief from my pain. I felt that he had made a very selfish choice that affected both of us. Why couldn't he just wait on God like I was doing? Even knowing how desperately he wanted a child did not give me any relief. I was in severe pain and could not for the life of me understand why God would allow another woman to give my husband the one thing I had desired to give him for almost ten years. Why would God allow us to get pregnant twice, but never have a baby to show for it?

How God? Why God? All I could hear in my spirit was, "And we know that God causes everything to work together for the good of those who love God and are called according to his purpose for them" (Romans 8:28 NLT).

What?!? Are you kidding me? But even though I couldn't feel it, even though I couldn't see how it was true. I knew that I had to trust God. No matter what it looked like, no matter how I felt, no matter what I could or couldn't see, I had to trust God!

I'm not going to say that it was easy, and I'm not going to say that I didn't have days that I struggled to get through, because I did and I do. But what I am going to say is even in this situation, God was and still is faithful. He is the healer and lover of my soul. He kept my heart and mind and still does. Even with all of the ups and downs, He was ALWAYS with me. God gave me the peace that I needed to get through this situation. Don't get me wrong, there were times I had to pray hard that God would help me get my emotions in check because I would be "all up in my feelings". But I never lost any sleep, I didn't stop eating nor did I over eat. But best of all, I experienced little or no feelings of loneliness. As John 14:18 (KJV) says, "I will not leave you comfortless: I will come to you." He didn't, and He did!

I couldn't imagine anyone having to go through this or any other difficult situation without God in their lives. As they say, my struggle was real and the pain ran deep. I never would have made it without God keeping and protecting me. I am glad that I had learned how to run to God during hard times, instead of running away from Him and blaming Him like I had done in the past. Thank You JESUS!

Your situation may not be this drastic or it could be even more drastic. Nevertheless, your pain is still real. Whatever your situation is today, whatever the condition of your marriage, before you decide to throw in the towel—seek God for your specific instructions and direction. Don't allow the enemy, your friends or family to advise you on what only God should be advising you on. Genesis 18:14 (NLT) asks the question, "Is anything too hard for the Lord?" My answer to that is a resounding NO! And your answer should be the same.

Notes

_____

_____

_____

_____

_____

_____

_____

_____

_____

_____

_____

_____

_____

_____

_____

_____

_____

_____

_____

Why Choose to Wait?

I INITIALLY CHOSE to wait for my husband to come back home because I loved my husband and because I didn't want another failed marriage. Most importantly, my commitment wasn't only to my husband, I also had made a commitment to God and I didn't take that commitment lightly. There are times that we give up too easily, not allowing God the time He needs to take care of our situations.

We may have different reasons as to why we choose to wait. But the one reason most of us may have in common is we don't want to feel like we are failures. Some of us don't want our friends or family members to be able to say to us, "I told you so."

I knew I was to wait because I found peace in not making a rushed decision to file for a divorce. I had learned how to stop making emotional choices but instead to seek God for answers in every situation of my life. So, I chose to wait.

I don't know how the wait will turn out in relation to my marriage; but what I do know is that if I wait on God for my answer, I can never go wrong! "Wait on the Lord: be of good courage, and he shall strengthen thine heart: wait, I say, on the Lord" Psalms 27:14 (KJV).

Notes

_____

_____

_____

_____

_____

_____

_____

_____

_____

_____

_____

_____

_____

_____

_____

_____

_____

_____

_____

_____

_____

_____

_____

_____

_____

_____

_____

_____

_____

_____

_____

_____

_____

_____

_____

_____

_____

_____

_____

_____

Is It Worth It to Wait?

THE ANSWER TO this question is one that we all will have to search our hearts to find. Some will say yes, some will say no, and others will be unsure.

I felt like my husband was worth waiting for because I loved him. I felt that God had put us together. I started out waiting on my husband to come back home. I waited on him to realize what he was losing, what he would be missing out on by leaving me. ME?? A treasure from God, his "Good Thing." WHAT? Because we all think that we are the best and only woman in the world for our husbands, right? And we should be.

What I realized was that as time passed, I had actually stopped waiting on him and began to wait on God to tell me what I should do. I waited to hear from God if this relationship, this marriage was truly ordained by Him and whether or not I should wait, stay or go. At this point, I wasn't so sure that my husband was worth waiting for, but I knew beyond a shadow of a doubt that God is well worth the wait.

Notes

_____

_____

_____

_____

_____

_____

_____

_____

_____

_____

_____

_____

_____

_____

_____

_____

_____

_____

_____

_____

_____

_____

_____

_____

_____

_____

_____

_____

_____

_____

_____

_____

_____

_____

_____

_____

_____

_____

_____

_____

What to Do
While You Wait?

WHAT WE SHOULDN'T do is blame ourselves for their leaving because it is a choice they made, nor should we try to manipulate our husbands into coming back to us by playing games, making threats or by using our children as pawns. We shouldn't run out and get into other relationships to get back at them because of what they have done. We also shouldn't blame them for everything. If we are honest, most, if not all of us, have our part in this play as well.

Now, don't get angry. I'm not saying it's our fault. But what I am saying is sometimes we lose sight of the things we do because we are so focused on what they are doing. This is a time to seek and ask God to search our hearts to see if there is anything that we have been saying or doing that may need to be corrected.

When my husband first decided to leave, I tried to convince him to stay. And then, once he had left, I tried to convince him to come back. I tried to hold on to him for dear life but it didn't work.

I was angry with God. What? YES! I knew that God had put us together and how in the world could or would He allow this to happen to me?

Once I got up off the floor from throwing my temper tantrum, I began to seek God for my answer. I also sought Godly counsel from my church elders. I learned that when you are going through something like this, it is not wise to seek counsel from a lot of different places. I told very few people and found that even some of my Christian friends said, "Girl, I wouldn't be going through all that. I wouldn't be waiting on him; I would be moving on."

If you are not a part of a local church, I urge you to seek God to help you to find a ministry that can give you some spiritual guidance. Because if we aren't careful, we can end up making the wrong decision and choices by listening to ungodly counsel.

What we have to realize is that our friends and family counsel us out of their emotions, out of their love for us. They don't want us to have to go through hurt and pain. And no, love isn't supposed to hurt; however, sometimes God allows us to experience certain trials because we have lost focus on our first love—HIM. And there is no one, not one person, on this Earth that can or will love us more than God.

We have to learn, as we wait, how to rest in God's presence, rest in His peace. We have to cry out to Him when we are in pain and going through, trusting that He hears our cries and will answer us. "Many *are* the afflictions of the righteous; But the Lord delivers him out of them all" (Psalms 34:19 NKJV).

When we make up our minds to wait, we have to be determined not to be double-minded. Today, he's being nice, said something nice, bought me something nice or just stopped by to say hello. So, it's all good. Everything is great and going according to our plans, so we are happy. But then tomorrow, he doesn't do any of those things and he doesn't even call. So now, we are on that downward part of the rollercoaster ride. We get angry and tell God, "You know what, never mind! Let him go on about his business." And we make up our minds to "find" someone else to take his place. But instead, we should make up our minds to wait, not on him to act right, but on God to move. We need to get in our secret place, our War Room, and pray.

If you haven't set up a War Room or War Closet, I would strongly recommend that you do. If you don't have the space to make a War Room or Closet, designate a specific spot in your home as your prayer place. The place where you sit and talk to and with God. We have to seek God sincerely with our whole hearts for His direction, allowing God to keep our hearts and minds. We must trust Him to give us the ability to be stable in every situation and not to be moved by the good or the bad that has been done to us, which is no small feat for most of us. "Let us hold unswervingly to the hope we profess, for He who promised is faithful." (Hebrews 10:23 NIV) Merriam-Webster defines unswervingly as, "without swerving or turning aside; steady." Also, it defines steady as, "direct or sure in movement; not easily disturbed or upset." The only way we are able to do any of these things is through God. Philippians 4:13 (NKJ) says, "I can do all things through Christ who strengthens me." He can and will give us the strength necessary not to be moved by what someone else does or does not do.

We need to make sure that while we wait, we are not only doing but also saying the right things. If we are trusting God to restore our marriages, we have to speak life into our marriages, speak life into our husbands. We cannot continually speak negatively or badly about our husbands and marriages and expect things to be good or to go like we want them to go. We have what we say and our words form our world. We have to start speaking what we desire and not what we see or are experiencing. "Death and life are in the power of the tongue: and they that love it shall eat the fruit thereof" (Proverbs 18:21 KJV). Choose to speak LIFE into your situation today.

What I have learned while waiting on God is that it wasn't so much about fixing my marriage, but more about what God needed to deal with that was in me. I began to realize that the wait for me is more about my understanding that it wasn't that God didn't want my husband and I to have a child or that He didn't want my marriage to work. It was more about His wanting me to love and desire Him more than anyone or anything else, even above any promises that He made to me. That's right, more than my husband or marriage and more than the babies we lost, He wanted me to love Him just for being who He is to me, my Savior—the great I AM—and not for the things that I knew that He could provide and give me.

Notes

_____

_____

_____

_____

_____

_____

_____

_____

_____

_____

_____

_____

_____

_____

_____

_____

_____

_____

_____

_____

_____

_____

_____

_____

_____

_____

_____

_____

_____

_____

_____

_____

_____

_____

_____

_____

_____

_____

_____

_____

_____

_____

When Is the Wait Over?

THE WAIT WILL be over for each of us at different points in our journey. We will either choose to stop waiting on our own or we will choose to continue to wait on God to tell us when the wait is over. What I desire most is that you get your instructions from God and not from anyone else, including yourself.

As for me, the wait isn't over until God says it is over. But I no longer am waiting on my husband to wake up and realize that he had a treasure in me. I am waiting on God to give me His instructions for my situation. I am waiting for Him to say "released" or for

Him to restore. We can avoid some disasters when we wait on God's instructions before we make a move or a decision.

But now as I wait, my focus is no longer on my husband, where he is or what he is doing. My focus is on God and where He is and what He is doing in me!

Notes

_____

_____

_____

_____

_____

_____

_____

_____

_____

_____

_____

_____

_____

_____

_____

_____

_____

_____

_____

_____

Restored or Released?

GOD IS THE Restorer and, in some cases, our marriages will be restored. On the other hand, some of us will be released from our marriages. If this is the case for you, it does not have to be a bad or sad time for you because you are released to be in a relationship with God. Don't look at it only as an ending but look at it as a beginning of a relationship with someone who will never leave you or forsake you! And for others, we will continue to wait until we receive clear instruction from God.

No matter what His answer is for you, know that to God, you are not a failure.

You cannot fail because He will not allow you to fail. Return to your first love. Get to know Him more intimately. Let Him be your husband during this period of waiting. "For your Creator will be your husband; the Lord of Heaven's Armies is his name! He is your Redeemer, the Holy One of Israel, the God of all the earth" (Isaiah 54:5 NLT).

Notes

_____

_____

_____

_____

_____

_____

_____

_____

_____

_____

_____

_____

_____

_____

_____

_____

_____

_____

_____

_____

_____

_____

_____

_____

_____

_____

_____

_____

_____

_____

_____

_____

_____

_____

_____

_____

_____

_____

_____

_____

Help While You Wait

FOLLOWING ARE A few scriptures for you to stand on as you wait and seek God for your answer. I also suggest two free inspirational applications that can be downloaded on your phone, iPad, Kindle or computer. "First 5", helps you spend the first five minutes of your day reading God's Word, and "Daughters of the King", which is a daily devotional for women. You may even want to consider going on a fast. Let God lead you as to what type and for how long. "So we fasted and petitioned our God about this, and he answered our prayer" (Ezra 8:23 NIV).

Whatever you do, I admonish you to search God's Word to find answers and directions, not just for this situation, but for every situation of your life.

Here are a few scriptures to get you started:

Psalms 40:1

Zechariah 11:11

Micah 7:7

Proverbs 20:2

Isaiah 40:31

Psalms 37:34

Psalms 130:5

Zechariah 11:11

Lamentations 3:25–26

2 Thessalonians 3:5

Notes

_____

_____

_____

_____

_____

_____

_____

_____

_____

_____

_____

_____

_____

_____

_____

_____

_____

_____

_____

_____

_____

_____

_____

_____

_____

_____

_____

_____

_____

_____

_____

_____

_____

_____

_____

_____

_____

_____

_____

_____

_____

_____

Conclusion

YOU DON'T HAVE to wait to seek God until you have tried everything and everyone else and it or they have failed you. God is faithful and He never fails. "But seek first his kingdom and his righteousness, and all these things will be given to you as well" (Matthew 6:33 NIV).

And just because things have not turned out the way we would have liked or hoped or even prayed that they would that doesn't mean God has failed us. It just means that He knows better what we need. As stated in Jeremiah 29:11 (KJV), "For I know the thoughts that I think toward you, saith the Lord, thoughts of peace, and not of evil, to give you an expected end."

So, for some of us, the questions still remain: Wait …? Stay …? Go …? We will not all get the same answer from God but in order to get the right answer for you, you will have to seek God with your whole heart. Allow God and not your emotions to determine which answer is right for you.

My prayer for every woman who reads this book is that you now know that you are not alone and no longer have to suffer in silence for fear of what others will think. I pray that no matter how God answers, you will develop a more intimate relationship with Him. I also pray that you will allow Him to love you like no one else can so that He can begin the healing process to get you through your test until your specific answer comes.

Allow God and God alone to get the glory out of your situation. God bless you as you continue to seek the One that is faithful to answer all of our prayers! "Who is like you, Lord God Almighty? You, Lord, are mighty, and your faithfulness surrounds you" Psalms 89:8 (NIV).

Notes

_____

_____

_____

_____

_____

_____

_____

_____

_____

_____

_____

_____

_____

_____

_____

_____

_____

_____

_____

_____

_____

_____

_____

_____

_____

_____

_____

_____

_____

_____

_____

_____

_____

_____

_____

_____

_____

_____

_____

About the Author

DONNA R. MARTIN, also known as Rene', is a blogger, speaker and, with the writing of this book, a published author. Her blog, "God's Way", teaches others how to seek God for answers to their problems and to apply the Word of God to their everyday situations.

Donna is a prayer warrior and intercessor who knows the need of being connected to God and the power of studying His Word.

She is a true worshiper. Donna is an active member of New Life Church of God in Christ in Montgomery, Alabama, under the pastoral covering of Dr. Terry Ellison and Lady Jevonnah Ellison. She now serves faithfully at the Church's Annex 5 location, initially under the teaching of Elder Eric L. Lee and now under the leadership of Co-Pastor Lois G. Russell. Donna is the daughter of Donald and Shirley Martin and has two brothers. She is the mother of three children, has two stepchildren and is a grandmother of eight. She is a graduate of the University of Alabama in Birmingham with a bachelor's degree in Health Information Management. She has worked for a well-known health insurance company for more than 33 years.

Ways You Can
Follow the Author

www.donnarenemartin.com

www.Facebook.com/DonnaRMartinEnterprises

www.linkedin.com/in/donna-martin-099b58148

@drenemartin

References

"unswervingly." Merriam-Webster.com 2016.
https://www.merriam-webster.com (October 2016)

"steady." Merriam-Webster.com 2016.
https://www.merriam-webster.com (October 2016)

A free ebook edition is available with the purchase of this book.

To claim your free ebook edition:

1. Visit MorganJamesBOGO.com
2. Sign your name CLEARLY in the space
3. Complete the form and submit a photo of the entire copyright page
4. You or your friend can download the ebook to your preferred device

Morgan James BOGO™

A **FREE** ebook edition is available for you or a friend with the purchase of this print book.

CLEARLY SIGN YOUR NAME ABOVE

Instructions to claim your free ebook edition:
1. Visit MorganJamesBOGO.com
2. Sign your name CLEARLY in the space above
3. Complete the form and submit a photo of this entire page
4. You or your friend can download the ebook to your preferred device

Print & Digital Together Forever.

Snap a photo

Free ebook

Read anywhere